Table of conter

Preface

In the present day many projects, programmes and portfolios suffer from a lack of accuracy built on false assumptions. In fact there is a whole movement which ignores the fundamentals in favour of the new and fashionable. Management of outcomes, stakeholders, benefits, value and governance are the New Jerusalem apparently. In focusing on the 'What' they lose sight of the 'How'. They are houses built on sand.

The devil is not in the detail. It is in the schedule. Always check the schedule. It will provide clues to identify what is wrong or right. If the schedule is wrong then the project is wrong and no amount of far-end management will fix it.

A common framework to carry out this fundamental work is now in your hands. This work has been inspired by the APM Earned Value Compass and may be used in conjunction with it. The Planning SIG, now known as the Planning Monitoring and Control SIG has rolled its sleeves up and gone back to basics.

I am delighted and reassured that David Birch Head of Programme Controls for the Olympic Delivery sees it as a valuable addition to the toolset.

Please use it and you must let us know how you get along. Your feedback is essential for improvements based upon experience.

Steve Wake
APM Planning Monitoring and Control SIG Chairman

Foreword

With around fifty individual projects making up the venues and infrastructure for London 2012 the challenge was to create and integrate a suite of schedules to avoid any surprises during delivery. With an immovable deadline and the highest possible level of public scrutiny, achieving this High Level Plan was one of the key challenges laid down for the delivery team.

Ultimately the requirement was to create and maintain an integrated suite of schedules that allowed programme-level decision making to be effective. These schedules progressively matured, allowing sequencing to be prioritised to minimise overall programme risk. At a tactical delivery level, delays on one project could be assessed to determine any impact on others, and gains could be reviewed to identify opportunities to accelerate follow on works.

Critically, the programme-wide perspective concentrated senior management effort in the most important areas of the programme. Direction was focused on areas which drove overall delivery, critical paths were actively managed and, where prudent, delays were accepted in areas with sufficient float.

It was recognised that the maturity of the schedule depends upon many factors including the size and complexity of the project, and that the maturity of each element of each schedule, and the overall programme, would vary throughout the delivery lifecycle.

Regular monthly project reviews and an assurance regime were implemented from an early stage in the programme. These were successful in driving project teams into a focused schedule maturity development cycle which, in turn, led to growing trust in status updates and an honesty in forecasting which allowed effective (and sometimes necessarily rapid) decisions to be made.

Overall, this approach ensured that the construction schedule set out in early 2007 was successfully delivered within the overall target dates; with completion of the so-called 'Big Build' on 27 July 2011, one full year before the Olympic Games Opening Ceremony. It also contributed significantly to minimising delivery costs.

Looking back, while the team did manage to guide, support and control the effective delivery of the programme, a scalable 'off the shelf' maturity matrix that could be adapted to every project would have been a valuable addition to the programme toolbox and may have enabled earlier identification of maturity status issues and for an even better result.

Now as a result of the considerable efforts of the APM Planning SIG; client organisations and programme and project teams no longer need to define schedule evaluation criteria from scratch. Instead they can readily select the required level of schedule maturity and the actual level achieved using this document as a basis. Clear guidance and the glossary remove any ambiguity about the meaning of certain terms (a common pitfall, especially for teams brought together from several organisations to deliver a programme).

At last there is a simple standardised tool that should provide a tangible way of demonstrating how good the schedule is and communicating how good it needs to be.

David Birch
Head of Programme Controls ODA Delivery Partner CLM

Acknowledgements

The Scheduling Maturity Model was developed by a sub-group of the APM Planning, Monitoring and Control (PMC) SIG, with contributions from Ken Sheard, Mike Semmons, Laura Smith, Mike Prescott, Jonathan Crone, Paul Kidston, Stephen Jones, Debashish Sarkar, Guy Hindley, Neil Curtis, Yetunde Adeshile, Thanos Tsourapas, Jenn Browne, Rebecca Smith and Alex Davis.

"The PMC SIG is most grateful to BAE Systems, which made its 'Project Control Maturity Framework Part A: Planning and Scheduling' document available to the SIG. This formed the base from which the APM PMC SIG developed this Scheduling Maturity Model. The intellectual property rights in the original 'Project Control Maturity Framework Part A: Planning and Scheduling' document remain vested in, and the property of, BAE Systems."

Review and testing of this Maturity Model has been conducted by the PMC SIG members and volunteers from a number of industry sectors – with positive feedback in all cases thus far. The authors would like to thank all for their help in making the Scheduling maturity model a reality.

Applicability

The Scheduling Maturity Model is intended to be applicable to schedules and scheduling processes for projects of all sizes in all industry sectors. It may be used in conjunction with the APM's Earned Value Compass [1] on which it is based and with which it shares a common goal: the use of the model as a decision support tool. The model should be scaled and tailored to the project concerned. For example, small scale projects may not need large amounts of schedule detail or risk analysis, so high-level schedules (e.g. "level 1" or "level 2") may be sufficient. Larger and more complex projects are likely to require lower-level scheduling (e.g. levels 3, 4 or 5).

Introduction

How do you measure an organisation's ability in implementing and applying a scheduling process across its projects? How do you know that your organisation's scheduling process is applied in a consistent and appropriate manner? For example, what are the minimum requirements needed to enable a project or programme to claim it has a robust scheduling process? How do you know your potential alliance partner, prime contractor, client or subcontractor has a robust scheduling process and its constituent elements are in place to ensure that either a project or programme can be controlled and delivered within known constraints?

The scheduling maturity model provides a step-by-step means to understand the 'as is' condition and reference it against a 'to be' condition for a number of scheduling process and quality attributes. The model uses a common framework and can be used for the assessment of a single project or programme's schedules, or to benchmark and compare the relative scheduling strengths of various projects across an organisation. It gives assurors and reviewers a consistent method of assessing either a project's or programme's scheduling health. The model can therefore be used as part of a tailored assessment of either a project or programme, regardless of size, complexity or importance.

This document is intended to be used in conjunction with the Earned Value Management APM Guidelines [2] Introduction to Project Planning [3] and the Introduction To Project Control [4].

It should also be noted that this is a Scheduling Maturity Model, not a Planning Maturity Model. Although planning encompasses the scheduling discipline, the ability to define and measure an organisation's planning maturity is more difficult than being able to do the same for scheduling. As a result, this model is limited to scheduling maturity for projects, and where appropriate, programmes as well. A separate planning maturity model will be addressed in a later SIG publication.

Fundamental Concepts

The Scheduling Maturity Model is intended to provide a defined means of establishing and improving the scheduling capability as part of an organisation's project, programme or enterprise control processes. Moreover, it is intended to support project and programme teams and organisations by improving an important part of their overall project controls capability. One element of this controls capability is the scheduling process. Although such a process may differ between organisations, it is likely to follow the same key process elements to generate a schedule. Figure 1 highlights the main stages in creating a schedule. The Scheduling Maturity Model has been developed to ensure that the quality of scheduling output generated by following the scheduling process meets requirements. In addition, the model may also be used when the process itself needs improvement to ensure that the schedule quality improves.

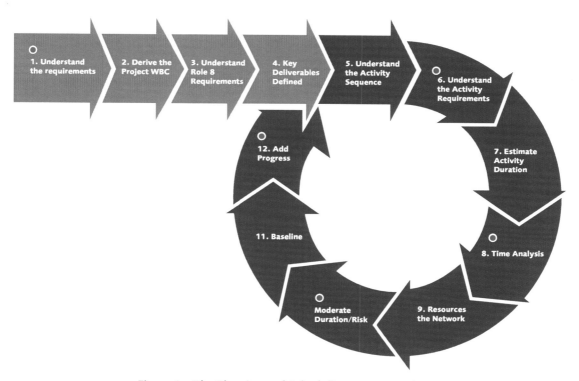

Figure 1 – The Planning and Scheduling process cycle

The project control processes, including scheduling, should be well understood throughout a mature project or organisation, usually through documentation and training. The processes should be continually monitored and improved. As a project or organisation gains in scheduling process maturity, it formalises its processes via policies, standards, and organisational structures. It also entails building an infrastructure and a corporate culture that support the methods, practices, and procedures of the project, programme or organisation so they endure after those who originally defined them have gone.

The maturity model is meant to be scaled and tailored to suit the size, scope, complexity and context of a particular project. Therefore, the assessment should take this into account when allocating a maturity level for a specific scheduling attribute within a particular stage in the project's lifecycle. Moreover, it is expected that some, if not all, maturity levels will change during the project's lifecycle; level 1 or 2 would be expected for most projects that have just started, even in organisations that have significant previous scheduling experience.

How is the Maturity Model used for Assessment?

In the context of this framework, the Scheduling Maturity Model is a comprehensive and systematic review of scheduling maturity. This can be used to aid process improvement by identifying shortfalls against the target standard.

The review is conducted using a maturity grid that outlines maturity levels against each attribute of the scheduling system, within a set of eight themes. The eight themes are colour coded in the spreadsheet used for the assessment. The 28 attributes are grouped as follows: Process & Toolset, Schedule structure & hierarchy, Schedule Integration, Schedule/Resource/Cost Integration, Schedule Risk, Schedule update and Maintenance, Environment and Scheduling Goal. A target maturity level should be established for the project or projects within an organisation at the outset and the maturity at the time of review related to this target. The target will typically be agreed with a customer of the project or within an organisation. It is for individual project teams/organisations to set their target standards. However, customers who require full compliance with a known standard (for example NEC3 and ANSI 748 as detailed in Annex C) are unlikely to be satisfied with maturity below level 3 during the implementation phase of a project.

The assessment process allows the project to clearly discern its strengths and areas in which improvements can be made, and should culminate in planned improvement actions which are then monitored for progress. The frequency of reviews is a decision for the project or organisation.

Throughout this document, the word enterprise has been used to encompass project, programme, portfolio, Business As Usual (BAU) and organisational activities. There are aspects of the model that are seen not to be enterprise-wide. Where a decision has been made to replace the word enterprise, this has been done using one or more of the adjectives used in the list above.

What are the Benefits?

Using the Scheduling Maturity Model for assessment should deliver a range of benefits, including:

- Identifying the organisation's scheduling strengths and areas for improvement.
- Providing a highly structured, fact-based, objective, consistent and repeatable approach to identifying and assessing a project's scheduling, and measuring progress periodically.
- Creating a common language and conceptual framework for the way you manage and improve scheduling on your project and, if applicable, other projects within an organisation.
- Educating people in your project on the fundamental elements of scheduling and how they relate to their roles and responsibilities.
- Involving people at all levels in process improvement.
- Ranking project scheduling maturity within an organisation or across the supply chain.
- Identifying and allow the sharing of best practice across projects within an organisation.
- Assessing and presenting the findings from a variety of scheduling reviews in a format that is easy to understand.
- Facilitating comparisons with other projects and programmes.
- Supporting the development of your business plan and strategy.

Assessment – The General Process

There is no single right way to perform the assessment using the maturity grid; the primary factors that determine the right approach for your organisation are its current culture and the desired outcomes from the assessment exercise. Different approaches deliver different benefits. Whichever approach is used, the key point to remember is that assessment is about the continuous improvement of your project.

Greatest value may be achieved from an assessment if it involves someone who has a working knowledge of the implementation and operation of a scheduling process. This ensures that the assessment can be completed with an understanding of the nuances between the different maturity levels for each of the attributes that are scored.

The assessment can be performed two different ways:

• Self-Assessment from within the project

• Independent Assessment – by Reviewers external to the project.

While the assessment is valuable the most critical phase of the process is action planning and implementation. Having completed the diagnostic phase, you may care to consider your response to the following questions:

• What identified strengths must we maintain to achieve maximum effect?
• What identified strengths do we develop and exploit even further?
• What identified areas for improvement do we acknowledge, but will not pursue because they are not key to our business?
• What identified areas for improvement do we acknowledge and see as paramount for us to address?
• How are we going to monitor progress against the agreed improvement actions?

The actions that are identified should be captured in a plan, with clearly defined responsibility and timescales for their implementation. To help with the prioritisation of the actions a grid such as that shown below may be of benefit.

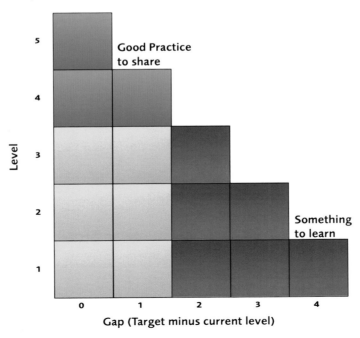

Figure 2 – Action Prioritisation

Implementation Roadmap – Maturity Levels and Stages

The structure of the Scheduling Maturity Model aims to reflect the stages that a project, programme or organisation will pass through when implementing a scheduling process. Progressing up from the foundations, it provides a logical path for the schedule process and its implementation. Should an organisation have little or no experience in scheduling, it should follow the roadmap in the order shown to maximise the benefits. However, if an organisation has more experience with scheduling, it is likely that the foundations and basics will already be embedded and so the focus may be on execution and the goal.

The stages are as follows:

1. **Scheduling foundations.** Establishing an effective scheduling process requires sponsorship and development and embedding of relevant competencies. It also requires that relevant scheduling roles and responsibilities are defined. Without these critical elements, a scheduling system is less likely to succeed.
2. **Scheduling basics**. The attributes in this stage form the main building blocks of an effective scheduling process. This maturity level is concerned with ensuring that these attributes meet the needs of the enterprise, with formal control of the schedule, and integration with the budget and resources, using a scheduling system that has defined processes.
3. **Execute the schedule.** Once the schedule has been developed to the point where it can be baselined, this maturity level is concerned with using the schedule to help manage the project or programme. In addition, this level is also concerned with efficiency of the scheduling system as well as effectiveness.
4. **Scheduling goal.** The ultimate maturity level is concerned with the use of the schedule, and the information it generates, as a decision support tool.

The model measures the maturity of the implementation attributes as a project establishes the basics, before starting to execute a scheduling process and finally using scheduling as part of a decision support tool. Once the assessment has been completed a profile is built up from the results. As the organisation's scheduling maturity evolves and improves, the profile from the eight themes will change. A suggested set of profiles is shown in figure 3.

The text on the vertical axes on each of the four maturity profiles in figure 3 relate to the titles of the 27 attributes that make up the Maturity Model. This text is too small to read; however, the emphasis is on the four stages, not the attribute titles. These profiles are based on the 'to be' output from the maturity model. Each attribute has its own colour and the overall profile relates to that particular stage. It should be noted that the colours are used to link the graphical output to each maturity theme (e.g. all eight attributes of schedule structure and hierarchy are orange) and the individual attribute within that particular theme (e.g. attribute 5 – 'basis of estimate' is also orange); the colours are not to be related in any way to performance. In addition, these profiles are suggestions only and are used only as a demonstration. Moreover, the maturity model output in the spreadsheet that accompanies this document has the 'as is' and 'to be' profiles on separate graphs for ease of use. A third graph has both series integrated together should this be required. Each organisation will have its own profile that may change as the project or programme evolves.

The idea is to develop the four stages for a project, programme or organisation at the appropriate time early in the lifecycle and agree the profiles with the key stakeholders. It is then necessary to ensure that regular reviews are held, using the maturity model outputs as a guide, to see if improvements in the quality of scheduling outputs have been made. Where this has not happened as expected, corrective action needs to be taken to ensure a desired level of maturity is not only reached, but embedded in the organisation.

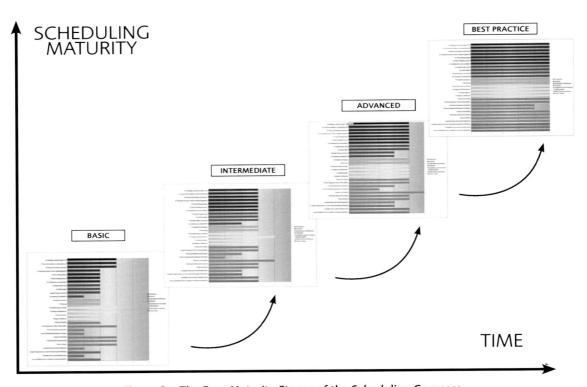

Figure 3 – The Four Maturity Stages of the Scheduling Compass

Scheduling Compass Guidance Information

Introduction

This section aims to provide guidance to support the use of the Scheduling Maturity Model assessment table. For each of the eight stages explanatory text is provided for the underpinning attributes. This text outlines:

- The Aim – the objective of the attribute
- The Reason – why the attribute is important
- Guidance information – additional information to assist users who are less familiar with the implementation and utilisation of Scheduling Processes and Systems.

Process and Toolset

Aim:
* To ensure that a consistent, documented scheduling process is applied to all projects within the enterprise. However with isolated occurrences of poor process performance which are resolved through corrective action plans. Where systemic issues are identified, the root cause is analysed and corrective actions implemented. The scheduling process is regularly reviewed to ensure compliance with requirements and improvements are identified and implemented.

Reason:
* Scheduling is often seen as either a new or optional process to a project or enterprise, however, inconsistencies in the scheduling process applied across projects will lead to difficulties in achieving a fully integrated master schedule. This would hinder the establishment of a robust critical path (or paths).

Guidance information:
* Implementing and sustaining a consistent scheduling process across project, programme, portfolio and enterprise is more likely where there is an organisation-wide, standard process that is understood and supported by all functions within the organisation in addition to a well disciplined scheduling function.

Attribute 2 – Scheduling tools are suited to enterprise needs

Aim:
* Management reporting information is directly available from the scheduling database in graphical format with the facility for drill-down of schedule metrics and other performance indices calculated against the scheduling data.

Reason:
* Reporting should be directly related to the state of the schedule as in the scheduling database. Any manual intervention is liable to increase the likelihood that the reporting may be out of date or out of alignment with the true schedule state of the programme and reduce the robustness of the reporting.

Guidance information:
* While the set-up costs of establishing a direct link from the schedule to the Management Information System (MIS) may be significant, the data will be a robust measure of the quality of the schedule data.
* Consideration should always be made as to whether the applied scheduling tool and links to MIS are appropriate for the level of complexity, integration requirements, volume of data and degree of communication of the schedule to meet all expectations of the enterprise without introducing excessive demands for creation and maintenance of the data.

Attribute 3 – Schedule analysis products are current and used throughout the enterprise

Aim:

- The output from analysis of the schedules should be up to date in accordance with the agreed update and reporting timescales. It should be reviewed as a part of the regular review meetings and should be the sole source of information for all schedule related decision making at all levels.

Reason:

- Schedule adherence is a critical element of managing any project, programme or Business As Usual (BAU) activities. As such, the data used to make schedule related decisions must be based on proper schedule analysis conducted against the sole, Integrated Master Schedule (IMS) that uses historical performance to predict future schedule performance.

Guidance information:

- The output from the scheduling process and toolset must satisfy the requirements of the enterprise in terms of currency of the data and level of detail provided. All schedule related questions must be answered by schedule analysis of the IMS. Stakeholders should not be permitted to create their own measures not directly linked to the schedule.

Attribute 4 – Defined organisation/roles & responsibilities

Aim:

- To ensure that the organisation is defined and that roles and responsibilities are documented, known and understood by all involved.

Reason:

- Having a clearly defined Organisational Breakdown Structure (OBS) and clearly defined and documented roles and responsibilities will bring clarity to the organisation responsible for delivery.

Guidance information:

- An OBS is used to give structure to the organisation responsible for delivering the project/programme. Roles and responsibilities are documented and known and understood by all participants. To provide greater clarity of responsibilities the OBS is mapped to the Work Breakdown Structure (WBS) to produce the Responsibility Assignment Matrix (RAM). The RAM clearly defines which part of the OBS has single point accountability for the delivery of the discrete element of the WBS.

Schedule Structure and Hierarchy

Attribute 5 – Capturing project and customer requirements

Aim:
* To ensure that the project and programme can satisfy all the customer requirements by translating these into a logical structure. The output of this part of the scheduling process creates a base-lined WBS. Any change to the scope is reflected through the WBS and managed through a documented change control process.

Reason:
* Thorough requirements capture is essential to ensure a robust baseline which satisfies the customer's and project's needs.

Guidance information:
* The project and customer requirements need capturing in a controlled and robust manner. Once captured they need to be managed through a documented, integrated change control process. The WBS is derived from the requirements capture process to ensure a consistency between the schedule delivery requirements and the customer requirements. Throughout the life of the project the requirements may evolve. It is vital that these changes are captured and when approved/authorised embedded into the WBS.

Attribute 6 – Basis of Estimate

Aim:
* To produce a robust estimate of the likely project/programme duration and cost. Estimating assumptions used are fully documented.

Reason:
* To produce a robust baseline for the project/programme. This estimate is fully bought into by all the stakeholders.

Guidance information:
* To produce a robust estimate all assumptions are documented. Ideally, previous project/programme historical data and/or parametric data has been used to help build the estimate with all relevant stakeholders engaged. The estimate, once assembled, has been reviewed as being fit for purpose by an independent authority. Throughout the life of the project the actual performance against the estimate is captured to help inform future projects and update the estimates library.

Attribute 7 – Deliverables defined and documented

Aim:
* To ensure that all deliverables are documented and clearly visible in the schedule.

Reason:
* All projects and programmes have deliverables. It is vital that these deliverables are clearly defined and visible to all by being integrated within the schedule.

Guidance information:
* The project's/programme's deliverables are clearly defined and documented. The deliverables are then managed and all changes are managed and fully documented. Key deliverables are integrated into the schedule logic, noting that some lower-level deliverables may be managed outside of the schedule, in accordance with local procedures. This enables a tracking through time of how achievement of the deliverables is progressing.

Attribute 8 – Structure of the schedule

Aim:
- To ensure that all the information in the schedule is comprehensively structured by the WBS.

Reason:
- To provide a logical structure to the schedule where all the data contained within the schedule, both activities and milestones, are assigned to the relevant part of the WBS.

Guidance information:
- The schedule is structured by its WBS. All activities and milestones are assigned to the appropriate WBS element within a single schedule. Within the IMS, all cross-WBS linkages are clearly defined between the appropriate activities.

Attribute 9 – Project scheduling and development of schedules

Aim:
- Schedules are developed in a comprehensive manner. The schedule is optimised and schedule risk items are highlighted. The schedule developed is approved by the management team.

Reason:
- To give confidence that the resulting schedule is developed in a comprehensive and consistent manner utilising appropriate techniques.

Guidance information:
- Schedule modelling techniques are used to help build the schedule. The initial schedule is built top-down and structured around the key milestones. These key deliverables are validated by detailed bottom-up planning and this demonstrates vertical traceability throughout the network. In the more advanced or mature schedule, resource optimisation is undertaken as a part of schedule development. A more mature schedule may also be used to identify and mitigate risk. Techniques may be used to help manage potential schedule-risk activities and ensure these areas are highlighted and brought to management attention.

Attribute 10 – Recurring schedule key characteristics

Aim:
- To ensure recurring elements of the schedule (e.g. production or a repeatable activity) are consistently applied across all projects/ programmes. Planning tools are utilised to optimise such activities across the enterprise.

Reason:
- To ensure that individual resource demands are optimised, managed and mitigated for both peaks and troughs across the enterprise.

Guidance information:
- Individual project/programme time and resource demands are captured for the enterprise. The demands for recurring element resources are optimised across the business to meet high-end analysis and reporting needs.

Attribute 11 – Detail of the schedule

Aim:
- A schedule that is logically structured at an appropriate level to clearly show all the work that is required to be undertaken. The schedule has stakeholder buy-in.

Reason:

- A schedule that is clearly structured in a logical manner and buy-in from all stakeholders has a much better chance of on-time, cost and quality delivery than one that has not.

Guidance information:

- The schedule needs to have a robust logic structured at an appropriate level of detail. The logical flow can be explained and understood by all stakeholders. The schedule is structured so that the detail can be rolled up for reporting purposes.

Schedule Integration

Aim:

* To ensure that it is understood how deliverables are related to milestones, how these are logically linked to activities and how the schedule drives all milestones.

Reason:

* It is essential that any project/programme can identify and document all its deliverables as schedule milestones. Such milestones are fully documented and logically linked to their relevant activities. All stakeholders must understand and agree to their description and know which deliverables they are accountable for.

Guidance information:

* The milestones should be derived from the WBS; this ensures that milestones relate to deliverables. Milestones can also relate to tangible, measurable events or 'gates' in a project/programme lifecycle. Milestones do not produce anything in themselves, but show a clear link between the end of one phase or stage and the start of the next. Documentation of milestones should include acceptance criteria and link this back to the relevant requirements. Moreover, the documentation should include milestone ownership and links to the assumptions, constraints and risks that directly relate to delivery.

Aim:

* To ensure that there is a single schedule, sometimes referred to as a Master Schedule or IMS, that is the definitive source for all related schedule, progress and resource information.

Reason:

* To enable all stakeholders to understand how their work, as captured in the relevant schedule(s), integrates into the IMS and how it contributes to achieving the overall output or outcome.

Guidance information:

- When generating an IMS, the hierarchy of schedules and their logical linkages needs to be captured. This ensures that all resource, progress and calendar information is held in one place. Reviewing progress at a single level, conducting 'what-if' analysis and impact analysis, and providing options/recommendations to the project or programme steering board can only be done efficiently and effectively if the schedules are linked together, both horizontally and vertically. Figure 4 illustrates how milestones from two different levels of schedule are linked horizontally and vertically into the IMS.

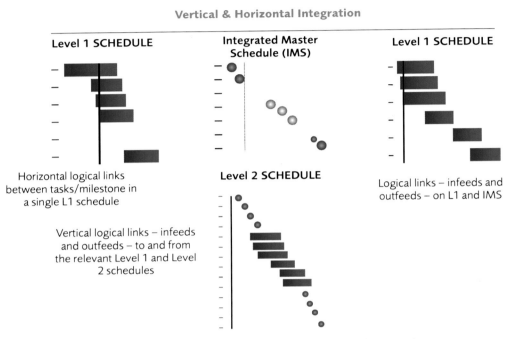

Figure 4 – An example of vertical & horizontal integration

Aim:

- To ensure that all activities and milestones in the schedule are logically linked and all deliverables are driven by both logic and activity progress, with all external dependencies captured and updated using the same process.

Reason:

- There is a need for a 'single source of truth' and a 'single point of integration' and a single schedule that can be used to make decisions and take action. This can only be achieved if the schedule has all its activities and milestones logically linked. In addition, it enables the identification of one or more critical paths and the amount and position of free and total float within the network. This is also true for all external dependencies; these must also be documented and linked in to the schedule, to ensure that progress on external activities that drive the schedule, or outputs that others depend on, are updated in accordance with the review and update cycle.

Guidance information:

- External dependencies are identified and collated in a discrete section within the schedule to aid identification. There should be no physical constraints on any milestone or activities, with the exception of those that have an explicitly documented and valid reason. The act of scheduling should ensure that all activities are logically driven; milestones are the result of actual activity achievement and not arbitrary events in time.

Aim:

- To ensure that one or more critical paths have been identified, and activity float has also been identified, calculated and optimised as a result of the scheduling process.

Reason:

- There is a need for a 'single source of truth' and the need to identify one or more critical paths and the amount and position of free and total float within the network. Activity float can be linked to the project/programme time-based Management Reserve (MR) and may be used to flex activities, between early and late dates, in line with the resource availability.

Guidance information:

- The schedule, once developed, must have at least one critical path identified, with defined rules regarding the use of positive and negative lag. The use of negative lag within the schedule should be avoided or discouraged. The schedule critical path(s) may alter once progress has been added. A documented schedule analysis process must exist and be used to determine changes to the critical path(s) and the ownership and control of float. As the schedule alters with progress updates to activities, the analysis process needs to be able to move float from one part of the schedule to another in a co-ordinated manner. This float optimisation process must also include a mechanism by which all stakeholders are informed of changes to the amount of float allocated to key milestones. The same mechanism must also ensure that float, where it forms part of MR, is not used to hide delays caused by other performance factors unrelated to the risks. Care must be taken that any 'risk buffer' allocated from Schedule Risk Analysis (SRA) is not added into the schedule prior to SRA.

Schedule/Resource/Cost Integration

Aim:
* To ensure that all activities are appropriately resourced, and that resources are in place and available when required. Resource demands have been optimised at the project, programme and enterprise level.

Reason:
* Resource availability is a key enabler of successful project/programme delivery. Without resources being available in a timely and cost effective manner the successful delivery of a project/programme would be compromised.

Guidance information:
* Resource demands are identified within the schedule. Appropriate resources can be assigned at a level appropriate to the project/ programme life cycle e.g. functional discipline, resource group or a named individual. Once identified, the available resources are then mapped to the project's requirements. Activities and resources are then optimised with appropriate adjustments made to the schedule. Resource optimisation continues throughout the life of the project/programme. Resource demands are balanced across the enterprise as necessary.

Aim:
* To ensure that timescales and costs are integrated at the appropriate level.

Reason:
* An alignment between cost and schedule ensures that project/programme control techniques can be applied to the schedule.

Guidance information:
* It is essential that schedule and budget baselines are synchronised. This provides a robust foundation for the project/programme financial control. The budgeting baseline is in alignment with the schedule resource demands.
* The detailed schedules are in full alignment and traceable to the Performance Measurement Baseline (PMB) and used for Earned Value Management (EVM) reporting on a regular basis. The PMB is established at an appropriate level for the size, complexity and cost of the project/programme.

Schedule Risk

Aim:

* To ensure that the risk management process is integrated into the scheduling process.

Reason:

* Integration between risk and scheduling is needed to ensure that confidence levels for time have been robustly generated using a risk schedule. The results are fed back into the deterministic (single point) schedule to derive schedule buffers for specific and non-specific Management Reserve; the latter is used to help manage emergent risks.

Guidance information:

* Integration of risk management to the schedule should centre on the following:
  o Ensuring the mitigation actions have been captured in the baseline.
  o Activity uncertainty ranges have been captured.
  o A process exists for generating a risk schedule from the IMS (deterministic) and selecting risks (and opportunities where appropriate) that can be linked to it.
  o A process for updating the risk schedule and IMS has been agreed and documented, along with the methods for determining changes to the schedule buffers and the update and drawdown of MR. More information on this may be found in the APM Guide to Interfacing Risk and Earned Value Management [5].

Schedule Update and Maintenance

Aim:

* To ensure that the process for collection and management of progress data is properly defined and that all reviews undertaken cover schedule compliance as part of their agenda. Projects and programmes must identify and manage variances and their impacts.

Reason:

* There is little value in recording and tracking schedule progress without comparing it with an agreed baseline. The baseline constitutes the target (in terms of time, scope and cost) against which schedule progress is measured. Using this measure performance can be assessed and it can be determined whether the project/programme is on time, on budget and within scope. Proper scope change management will result in baseline modifications, reflecting the project/programme current state and allowing accurate future progress and performance assessments.

Guidance information:

* A formal process for capturing scope change should be developed, documented and rolled out across the business, in a consistent way. Scope changes should be reflected in the baseline. A new baseline should be considered when a scope change occurs and may become the revised Performance Measurement Baseline (PMB). Ideally, all processes must be rigorously controlled and their application independently audited.

Attribute 20 – Schedule analysis

Aim:

* To ensure that schedule analysis is conducted on a regular basis to identify variances and produce recovery plans as appropriate.

Reason:

* Schedule analysis is fundamental in determining the position of project/programme with regards to time and cost. Key schedule parameters such as total and free float, critical path, interfaces, etc must be reviewed in order to understand whether the project/programme is performing to time and to budget. Early detection of variances must be addressed via predictive methods to produce recovery plans and bring the project/programme back on course.

Guidance information:

* In order to conduct any schedule analysis, there needs to be an appropriately resourced and logically linked schedule which identifies one or more critical paths, key activities and milestones. There must also be a baseline schedule against which progress and performance is measured. When either key activities or milestones are compromised, then the schedule must be analysed to identify remedial action(s) which can be developed to form a recovery schedule.

Attribute 21 – Schedule change control

Aim:

* To ensure that an integrated change control process exists. All project/programme changes are assessed for impacts to the schedule.

Reason:

* Schedule changes that are not documented, controlled or communicated can lead to confusion and jeopardise the success of a project/programme, with adverse consequences on cost and duration. A rigorous change control process that assesses the impacts of schedule change on various levels is required.

Guidance information:

- Schedule changes must be properly captured and documented. They must then be communicated to all stakeholders through a change control process. Before changes are adopted in the schedule, formal authorisation must be obtained through a formal change control process. A full history of changes should be maintained for audit purposes. For further detailed guidance on change control and baseline change management, please refer to the Earned Value Compass [1].

Environment

Attribute 22 – Scheduling roles and responsibilities

Aim:
- To ensure that the scheduling resources form an integral part of the project/programme team.

Reason:
- A specialist scheduling resource or planner should be responsible for the coordination, integration and management of the schedule. The planner should be in the loop with all details affecting the project progress and success, and should be left to drive the use and application of the schedule. A planner must also inform all stakeholders on all aspects of the schedule, through regular updates, that may adversely affect the successful execution of the project/programme.

Guidance information:
- The project/programme manager must put a lot of effort into integrating the project team, ensuring that all parties are involved and all details communicated, thus avoiding situations where the planner is left to work independently of the project team. The planner must be the project manager's right hand, and his role must be recognised as an equal partner in the project team. Finally a planner's role must not be viewed as purely for project reporting purposes – indeed there is a big element of reporting as a result of project/programme requirements, but there is also forward-looking planning, which should be the focus of the planner's work. Please see attribute number 4 which also deals with roles and responsibilities.

Attribute 23 – Project scheduling resources

Aim:
- To ensure that adequately trained and skilled scheduling resource, together with appropriate toolset(s) are available so that schedules are built and then utilised to ensure project/programme delivery.

Reason:
- To ensure that appropriate skilled resource is used to define, build and manage the schedule within relevant toolsets. The whole team buys into and understands the resource-scheduling process.

Guidance information:
- Appropriately skilled resource and toolset is applied to the integrated scheduling process. Lessons learnt from previous projects are fed into the project when forming new teams and planning resources/tools to be used. The whole team follows the planning process.

Attribute 24 – Team and manager buy in

Aim:
- To ensure that the whole team buys into the project schedule. There is one schedule. It is used by all engaged on the project. It is the single source of truth for the whole project.

Reason:
- To ensure the whole project team buys into and "owns" the project schedule. With one schedule proactive use is made fully effective.

Guidance information:
- Team and management engagement is essential to ensure that the project schedule is owned by the team. Visible and active senior management engagement with the schedule is a great enabler for gaining the whole team buy-in.

Attribute 25 – Stakeholder (customer, partner & supplier) engagement

Aim:
- To ensure that the project stakeholders are engaged throughout all stages of the project lifecycle with the project schedule.

Reason:
- The more engaged the stakeholders are with the project schedule, the more the project or programme will deliver what is required and meet the customer's objectives.

Guidance information:
- Engagement of the stakeholders throughout all stages of the project and schedule lifecycle is key. Summary schedules should be used to brief key stakeholders and gain their involvement with the planning and scheduling process. This engagement should be second nature so that customers, partners and suppliers are automatically involved in the scheduling development, baselining and update process.

Attribute 26 – Planning and scheduling competencies

Aim:
- To ensure that the project or programme team is suitably qualified and competent to undertake the duties required of them, both in scheduling and any toolset competencies.

Reason:
- Skilled individuals are worth their weight in gold. They have suitable knowledge and experience to undertake an efficient and thorough job.

Guidance information:
- Staff need to be appropriately trained in both planning and the toolset(s). To build on the scheduling competencies, courses and mutual self help workshops should be organised, to share experiences and gain knowledge to further enhance their skills across the wider project environment. This attribute should be read in conjunction with attributes number 4 and number 22, which look at roles and responsibilities.

Attribute 27 – The use of the schedule as a communications aid

Aim:
- The schedule is used by all to communicate the project's current position.

Reason:
- The schedule is regularly used to inform and stimulate project decision making across the whole project team.

Guidance information:
- To inform and ensure effective project and programme decision making, the schedule is used by all within the project/programme team and across the enterprise. The schedule is one of the key reporting mechanisms used to communicate project status information within the enterprise. The schedule is used to model "what-if" scenarios as a mechanism for proactive management, which may include change management and risk mitigation(s) update.

Attribute 28 – Scheduling as a decision support tool

Aim:
- To ensure that informed and up to date decisions are made with respect to project delivery by using the updated project schedule as a decision support tool.

Reason:
- The schedule conveys the current status and forms the basis for trend analysis against the baseline. Performance metrics originate from the time phasing of the schedule. The schedule is used as a basis from which to measure the effectiveness of, and plan the implementation of, corrective actions.

Guidance information:
- The schedule is the single point of reference for all time and resource phased information. Efficiency of progress updates enables the schedule to be relied upon as a measure for the effectiveness of corrective actions as necessary. Systemic issues and problem areas are addressed to prevent them re-occurring on this or other projects/programmes across the enterprise.

Annex A – Scheduling Maturity Model Questions

| | ATTRIBUTE MATURITY LEVEL | | | | | | |
	1	2	3	4	5	As Is	To Be
Process and toolset	**1. Use of Scheduling Process & compliance to contractual requirements**						
	The scheduling process is ad-hoc and not coordinated. There are no documented scheduling guidelines or standards. The schedule complies with most, if not all, applicable contractual requirements for schedules.	The scheduling process is ad-hoc and not fully coordinated. Some local scheduling guidance in place. The schedule complies with all applicable contractual requirements for schedules.	The scheduling process is structured and focused. It utilises a set of standard, documented, and controlled processes for the preparation and publication of schedules. Reviews/audits are periodically conducted to ensure documented processes are being followed and contractual requirements are being met.	The scheduling process is followed by the whole team. It utilises metrics to monitor the health of the scheduling processes and performs scheduled self-assessments, as documented, to ensure processes are being followed.	All projects and contracts within the programme adhere to a consistent documented scheduling process. All project teams follow the same process. Poor process performance is isolated, and corrective action plans are implemented. Root cause analysis is performed and corrective actions are implemented when scheduling process issues are identified. Process improvements are identified and fed into the Project Management Function.		
	2. Scheduling tools are suited to enterprise needs						
	Schedules are generated by hand or PC graphics software.	Master and team schedules are developed manually using one or more databases. Integration between team schedules is managed separately from the scheduling toolset.	Project management software (networking and resource loading capability) is used for non-recurring schedules or other appropriate schedules. Management-recognised standard software tools are used. All schedules are integrated in a 'single-source' database with manual links to other systems. Schedules are manually linked to other systems as part of performance management.	All schedules are integrated by automation into a 'single-source' database. There is automated linkage between the 'single-source' schedule database and other systems containing schedule data. Schedule performance metrics exist in the MIS. Appropriate scheduling tools are utilised based on the size and complexity of programme.	Colour-coded (or other differentiator) schedule metrics with drill-down capability are generated from the scheduling database for the MIS. Presentation graphics are generated from the scheduling database. Major supplier detailed schedule data is transmitted via electronic data interchange (or other automated technology) and is electronically integrated into the programme schedule. Scheduled/network templates are used for standard sequences of activities.		
	3. Schedule analysis products are current and used throughout the enterprise						
	Schedule update is ad-hoc. Clearly defined ownership of schedule elements is not always appropriate.	Schedules are updated and statused on a regular published update cycle per project management and contractual requirements. (Estimated/forecast dates are projected for milestones and activities which are past due or with negative float.)	Schedule performance metrics are prepared and reviewed with/by Team Leaders on a regular (or other documented) basis. (Examples include: Current schedule vs. actual milestones, deficient item listings, supplier status and impact of late items.)	The following types of metrics are also reviewed regularly. Examples include: an overall schedule performance summary/variance analysis; network and Critical Path Analysis. The project utilises float as an indicator of schedule health.	Predictive analysis is reported in regular meetings and is utilised in the decision-making process by the project management team.		

ATTRIBUTE MATURITY LEVEL							
	1	**2**	**3**	**4**	**5**	**As Is**	**To Be**
4. Defined organisation/roles and responsibilities							
	No consideration of an Organisation Breakdown Structure (OBS). Roles and responsibilities are not documented.	Roles are defined but responsibilities are not. No OBS is identified in the schedule.	All activities are assigned to an element of the OBS. A documented correlation exists between the WBS and OBS, utilising the RAM.	Organisational issues are subject to change control. OBS and RAM are maintained within the scheduling tool to reflect the current standard.	The project OBS includes cross-references to other OBS at the enterprise level.		
5. Capturing project and customer requirements							
	There are no formal methods for capturing customer requirements – e.g. WBS or only an outline WBS or PBS.	Scope is documented, defined and decomposed into meaningful, manageable elements. A recognised WBS is established.	All authorised work elements are defined for the project. A WBS is used in this process and captures the full scope of work.	A systematic process decomposes project requirements and identifies the scope of work necessary to deliver these requirements. The scope of work is under configuration control. The link between customer requirements and WBS elements is clearly defined.	All customer requirements have been decomposed into the WBS and associated work scope. This mapping is transparent and under configuration control. Changes to the technical baseline or requirements are properly managed through a documented, integrated change control process.		
6. Basis of Estimate							
	Project estimates are produced without Project Team consultation and without documented procedures.	There is a record of estimates but formal estimating techniques and processes have not been applied. Estimating assumptions are not fully documented.	A formal structured estimate has been generated following standard estimating procedures. All estimating assumptions are fully documented.	Estimates are based on previous project norms, historical data, or parametric estimating. All estimating assumptions are fully documented.	The estimate has been reviewed by an independent authority. Upon completion of projects the actual performance data is used to inform future estimates/update project norms. Full ownership and authorisation of the estimate is shared by all relevant stakeholders.		

Schedule structure and hierarchy (vertical label, left margin)

ATTRIBUTE MATURITY LEVEL							
1	**2**	**3**	**4**	**5**	As Is	To Be	
7. Deliverables defined and documented							
Project deliverables are not defined and are not referenced back to the objectives/WBS.	The project deliverables are defined, but not integrated with the WBS or schedule.	The project deliverables are clearly defined and documented and related to the WBS.	The deliverables are documented and defined and the outputs clearly visible in the schedule.	The project deliverables are documented, defined, and clearly visible in the schedule. Changes to the deliverables are managed and documented.			
8. Structure of the schedule							
There is no consideration of any structure. Activities are randomly placed in the schedule.	There is an attempt to structure the schedule by the WBS. Not all activities are assigned to a WBS element.	All activities are assigned to a WBS element.	The schedule is comprehensively structured by the WBS. Cross-WBS linkages are defined in the schedule logic.	All tasks and milestones are assigned to their relevant WBS. The schedule is comprehensively structured by the WBS and its different levels. Cross-project linkages are defined in the schedule logic.			
9. Project scheduling and development of schedules							
Some schedule constraints, calendars and major deliverables are identified.	All constraints, calendars and major deliverables are identified.	Durations and resource requirements are based upon demonstrated historical performance and are utilised in schedule development. A project planning checklist is used at the front end of the project to make sure all areas are being covered.	Schedule structure demonstrates improving project maturity and increasing identification of project risk. The schedule is developed top-down based on major events. Project milestones and deliverables are validated bottom-up, demonstrating vertical traceability. Suppliers provide detailed schedule information on development items. Schedule risks are identified. Issues of resource constraints can be identified and timely corrective action proposed.	Schedule modelling techniques are used (e.g., networking or manufacturing capacity analysis). All schedule optimisation techniques are documented along with a rationale and risk assessment and are approved by management. Schedule risk items are highlighted.			

Schedule structure and hierarchy – continued

ATTRIBUTE MATURITY LEVEL						As Is	To Be
1	**2**	**3**	**4**	**5**			

<table>
<tr><td colspan="8">10. Recurring schedule key characteristics</td></tr>
</table>

Schedule structure and hierarchy – continued

1	2	3	4	5	As Is	To Be
There is a master schedule which is driven by the programme top-level contractual requirements. Schedule requirements are managed in a standalone system.	Preliminary (immature) bill of material is available and is managed in an informal, undocumented system. Production/supply chain requirements are tracked independently of the schedule.	Recurring schedule demands are loaded manually into the production/supply chain system. Recurring schedule metrics are used to ensure "Build-To/ Buy-To/Support-To" packages are available as scheduled. Independent demands are utilised in the production/ supply chain system. Metrics (such as Line of Balance) are used to manage production/ supply chain system.	Independent demands are permitted but follow a strict, documented approval process prior to input to the production/ supply chain system. There are documented goals and improvement plans for overall lead-times and inventory levels (if applicable).	Enterprise planning is utilised to optimise schedules on the project. All enterprise production/ supply chain projects are integrated into the schedule and reporting tools to provide high-end analysis capabilities. Metrics are in place to ensure independent demands are limited.		

11. Detail of the schedule

1	2	3	4	5	As Is	To Be
The schedule contains little detail, just a few tasks and milestones. There is no confidence that the activities scope the entire project.	The schedule contains a mix of low-level and high-level activities. There are varying levels of confidence that the project can deliver within its constraints.	The schedule, though not fully documented, contains enough detail to manage the activities and give confidence to meet the committed timescales.	The schedule flows in a clearly visible, logical manner. Milestones are clearly linked and logically relate to the relevant activities. There is a high level of confidence in the project delivery dates and costs.	The schedule is clearly and competently structured at an appropriate level of detail. This detail can be clearly and logically explained by the task owners, CAMs, and project managers. The schedule gains stakeholder approval across all levels of the management structure. Schedule detail can be rolled-up to provide a summary for reporting purposes.		

Schedule integration

12. Integration of milestones

1	2	3	4	5	As Is	To Be
A limited rationale behind the milestones is identified. Milestones do not relate to any part of project delivery or schedule activities. Some key milestones are identified.	Deliverables are defined as milestones. Milestones are not fully documented. Key milestones have been identified.	Milestones clearly relate to deliverables. A clear definition of each milestone is documented. All key milestones that lie on the critical path have been identified.	Milestones are fully integrated into the activity logic of the underlying schedule. Customer 'gateway/ event' milestones are clearly identified as logical points in the schedule. Milestone documentation includes unambiguous acceptance criteria.	Management are fully committed to the milestones contained within the project schedule. The schedule drives all milestones. There is clear and unambiguous documentation of all milestones. Milestone outputs are agreed with their customers (internal and/or external).		

13. Schedule integration

1	2	3	4	5	As Is	To Be
Some scheduling requirements are defined to teams, partners, or suppliers. Schedules are developed in isolation.	Scheduling requirements are appropriately flowed to all teams and functions including major suppliers/partners.	Major team/function/ supplier/partner milestones and lead-times are incorporated into project schedules. Appropriate interfaces between teams have been identified and documented.	Teams have agreed to interface points (inputs and outputs) which demonstrate horizontal and/or vertical integration.	A single-source, integrated hierarchy of schedules is maintained. Where appropriate, detailed supplier development schedules are incorporated into team and project schedules. Data integration process is documented and maintained.		

	ATTRIBUTE MATURITY LEVEL						
	1	2	3	4	5	As Is	To Be
Schedule integration – continued	**14. Schedule logic/dependencies**						
	There is no logic in the schedule. Activities are held in place by constrained dates.	Some activity dependencies defined. Many tasks are not logically linked.	All activity dependencies are defined. No standalone activities are in the schedule. No negative logic links are used.	Activities are all placed in time by the critical path process. No "target/ fixed" dates imposed except for incoming external milestones.	Schedules are 100% logic-linked between all activities. All milestone dates are driven entirely by logic, the only exception being incoming external milestones, with full Critical Path(s) defined.		
	15. Critical Path and the use of float						
	There is no defined Critical Path. Float is not considered.	A limited Critical Path exists. Activities are constrained and negative float exists.	The longest path, which may be critical, has been identified. Some activities may have float.	Full Critical Path(s) exist in the schedule. All forms of float may be distributed throughout the schedule.	All forms of float are used to construct and justify the level of schedule Management Reserve. Float is optimised at all levels in the schedule. Multiple critical paths may have been identified within the schedule.		
Schedule/resource/cost integration	**16. Resourcing**						
	There are no resources on any of the activities.	The schedule includes some resourced activities. Resources that are "critical" to project delivery have been identified and allocated.	All activities have resources allocated to them. Stakeholders are aware of the resource demands that are placed upon them. Resource loading at the enterprise level including identification of internal and external resources and resource types (e.g. plant/ equipment/facilities).	The resourced project schedule is analysed and resources either levelled or smoothed to balance out resource requirements vs. resource availability.	Resource levelling/ allocation is used to manage resources at project, programme and enterprise level during schedule development/ maintenance. Resource optimisation is a continuous process, ensuring requirements are identified far enough into the future to meet allocation lead-times.		
	17. Schedule/cost integration						
	There exists no alignment between schedule elements and budget elements, either in terms of duration, time-phasing or value.	Schedule elements and budget elements map directly into a single integration point to create the Performance Measurement Baseline.	The project schedule is consistent with, and traceable to, the time-phased budgeting information in terms of duration and value.	Detailed schedules are directly traceable to values in the EVM/ Cost management reporting system.	Revisions to schedule and budget baselines are synchronised via the same change control process. The level of cost/schedule integration and change control is appropriate to the complexity, size and total project cost.		
Schedule risk	**18. Consideration of schedule risk**						
	No consideration of risk is made in the schedule.	Risk is considered, but no mitigation actions/strategies are documented in the schedule.	The schedule considers risk and uncertainty in the activities and documents how risk mitigation activities are addressed by the project.	Schedule Risk Analysis techniques are used within the project and provide confidence levels at project level. The risk process is fully considered when the schedule is built and fully integrated with the update process.	The risk process is fully embedded into the scheduling process. Schedule risk networks are used, with full traceability between the planning (deterministic) and the risk (probabilistic) networks to drive continuous improvement through the scheduling process.		

	ATTRIBUTE MATURITY LEVEL						
	1	2	3	4	5	As Is	To Be
Schedule update and maintenance	**19. Baseline progress and control**						
	Progress against the schedule is not collected.	The schedules are reviewed infrequently. Progress collection is sporadic and ad-hoc. Subjective systems are used for interpreting progress.	The information in the schedule is regularly reviewed and maintained as relevant, accurate and timely. A defined and agreed method of measuring progress is used. Progress is collected on a regular basis and the schedule updated. A baseline schedule exists. (The baseline schedule and all changes to it are approved by the applicable team or functional leaders and programme management.)	Progress is recorded and managed against the baseline. A system that manages achievement against planned targets is used throughout the project lifecycle. A regular review cycle is in place that synchronises schedule and cost information. All scheduling meetings consider the schedule and identify progress and changes against the baseline.	Processes for progress collection and management are defined. All project reviews include schedule compliance on their agenda. Impact of project and programme issues are identified and managed. Lessons learned are taken from these reviews and spread to other teams and fed back into the scheduling process.		
	20. Schedule analysis						
	There is irregular and/or inconsistent analysis of the schedule and it is not communicated to senior management. Progress is largely based on milestone counting.	Schedule analysis is based on a review of current/forecast only. No reference to performance against the baseline is made.	Schedule Variance Analysis is performed on current schedule vs. baseline and provided to management. Recovery recommendations are made to management based on variance analysis. Schedule interdependencies are identified and schedule analysis is conducted to determine critical path for non-recurring and workflow for recurring work. A documented, disciplined process is used to identify and assess schedule risks. Recovery plans are prepared when a major milestone or control point is impacted and status is monitored against the recovery plan.	Perform predictive analysis such as network, Critical Path and float analysis to determine programme pacing items and trends to focus management attention on potential problems. Regular audits of the schedule are conducted to produce metrics to test schedule robustness.	Schedule Risk Analysis (SRA) methodologies are used to quantify schedule risk. Formal SRA is performed and used in the decision-making process. Formal recovery plans are prepared when network float to a future major milestone or control point is negative.		
	21. Schedule change control						
	Schedules are changed without documentation, control or communication.	Changes to schedules are communicated through the organisation and stakeholders in an ad-hoc manner.	The project has a formal baseline schedule change control process which requires approval on all substantive changes. (The schedule change control documentation clearly explains the reason for the change and quantifies the change.) The project clearly follows the schedule change control process. Schedule changes for interface points are documented and controlled. Risk is addressed in the change control process.	An integrated change control process exists. All project changes are assessed for impacts to the schedule.	The schedule change control process is integrated with an enterprise change control or "awareness" process to determine impact and resources affected throughout the enterprise (business unit, site, project, programme).		

ATTRIBUTE MATURITY LEVEL						
1	2	3	4	5	As Is	To Be
22. Scheduling roles and responsibilities						
The planners' roles and responsibilities are not defined.	The planners' roles and responsibilities are defined, but not understood or appreciated by the wider team.	Stakeholders fully buy in to the planners' roles and responsibilities. The responsibility for coordination, integration, and management of the overall schedule is clearly allocated to a single function or team. The planners are embedded as part of the project team under the direction of the project manager.	All stakeholders have input into the schedule in a coordinated manner under the direction of the planners. The planners are automatically invited to all meetings considering the schedule and actively involved in the decision-making.	Planners are fully integrated into the project team. Their advice is sought to work definition and schedule issues.		
23. Project scheduling resources						
The number of resources and/or skill levels are inadequate to meet project requirements. Necessary tools and training are unavailable. Management support is lacking for scheduling processes.	Adequate resources are available to meet project requirements. Adequate training and skill level for implementation of basic scheduling tools and techniques is provided. Management is generally supportive of the scheduling processes.	The necessary training and tools are available to meet project requirements. User guides and procedures are documented, accessible, and being used. All stakeholders have input into the schedule. The planning team can draw upon previous implementation experience.	There exists adequate training and skill level for implementation of advanced scheduling tools and techniques. All stakeholders have input into the schedule, and input and outputs are scrutinised, coordinated and understood.	Skilled and highly trained resources are assigned. Management fully supports the integrated scheduling processes. Continuous process improvement is actively pursued. The planning process is bought into and followed by the whole team. Lessons learnt from previous projects are fed into new projects when forming new teams.		
24. Team and manager buy-in						
There is no management buy-in for involvement in the creation of the schedule. Planners create schedules in isolation. There is negligible senior management understanding of the schedule.	A degree of team member and management buy-in to the schedule exists. The schedule is used to brief management and colleagues.	Team members use the schedule and actively contribute to reviews. Managers use the schedule. All stakeholders have input into the schedule.	All managers and team members buy in to and use the schedule. Senior management frequently uses the schedule and advocates its proactive use. Senior management is involved in the generation, agreement, and control of the schedule.	The schedule is owned and supported by all project team members. It is referred to as "the project schedule, created by the team".		
25. Stakeholder (customer, partner and supplier) engagement						
Stakeholders are not identified. There is no stakeholder involvement in project scheduling.	An initial list of stakeholders is generated. Stakeholders are infrequently involved in project scheduling.	Stakeholders are consulted in the identification of the WBS, deliverables, schedule, and resultant milestones. Frequent interaction with stakeholders is the norm.	All stakeholders are thoroughly integrated into the planning and scheduling process. Stakeholders are managed and included as part of the team. Summary plans are used to brief stakeholders. Stakeholders are formally involved at regular, documented review points, and are involved in setting the baseline.	Stakeholder engagement in planning and scheduling is custom and practice.		

Environment

	ATTRIBUTE MATURITY LEVEL						
	1	**2**	**3**	**4**	**5**	**As Is**	**To Be**
Environment – continued	**26. Project scheduling resources**						
	Planners/core project management team have generally received no training and are inexperienced in either the planning discipline or toolset.	Inconsistent training is provided to those involved in scheduling. Training is generally focused only on the toolset. Schedulers have limited experience in the discipline and toolset.	Adequate experience exists within the planning team. Planning team members have received training. Advanced training is available (including EVM, advanced scheduling, project management).	All project team members are trained to an appropriate level of competence in both scheduling and toolset skills. Training and competency records are maintained.	Planners develop courses and workshops to enhance planning and toolset skills. LFE (Learning From Experience) functions are held and planners regularly attend and contribute. The enterprise is adequately trained and competency records maintained.		
	27. The use of the schedule as a communications aid						
	The schedule is not used to communicate the status of the project to stakeholders.	The schedule is used as an informal aid to communicate project status to some stakeholders. Feedback is not always asked for or acted upon.	The schedule is formally used to communicate project status to all stakeholders and distributed on a regular basis.	The schedule is used to inform stakeholders of options to stimulate informed decision-making. Action plans are defined and delivered.	The schedule is used to communicate project status at the enterprise level, in order to stimulate informed decision-making across the enterprise.		
Scheduling goal	**28. Scheduling as a decision support tool**						
	Scheduling data is not used to support formal project reviews.	Scheduling data is used in an inconsistent and irregular manner to support formal project reviews. Management has a limited ability to use the schedule to help make informed decisions.	Scheduling data forms a key element of a regular, formal project review. Responsible managers can explain the cause and impact of deviations from the baseline triggered by exceeding management-set thresholds.	Responsible managers review trends, performance indices and VARs to regularly inform recovery planning and scheduling and to determine required future performance levels and associated resource requirements. The variance is used to inform recovery action plans being created and integrated into the baseline.	Efficacy, efficiency, and effectiveness of corrective actions and management decisions are measured as part of the management feedback loop. Responsible managers address systemic and systematic problem areas and address these to prevent them reoccurring across other projects, programmes and at enterprise level.		

Annex B – Glossary

Activity. An element of work performed during the course of a project. An activity normally has an expected duration, an expected cost, and expected resource requirements. Activities are often subdivided into tasks.

Acceptance criteria. A prioritised set of criteria that the project product must meet before the customer will accept it, i.e. measurable definitions of the attributes required for the set of products to be acceptable to key stakeholders.

Baseline. See Performance Measurement Baseline.

Benefit. The measurable improvement resulting from an outcome perceived as an advantage by one or more stakeholders.

Budget. The resources (in money and/or hours) assigned for the accomplishment of a specific task or group of tasks.

Buffer. A term used in critical chain Also used in the risk management sense for contingency allocated to a schedule after confidence modelling has been conducted.

Business As Usual (BAU). One or more repeatable activities that relate to the day-to-day operation of a company or organisation.

Change control. A process that ensures that all changes made to a project's baseline scope, time, cost or quality objectives are identified, evaluated, approved, rejected or deferred.

Critical Path (CP). A sequence of activities through a project network or schedule from start to finish, the sum of whose durations determines the overall project duration. There may be more than one such path. The path through a series of activities, taking into account interdependencies, in which the late completion activities will have an impact on the project end date or delay a key milestone.

Customer*. The person or group who commissioned the work and will benefit from the end results.

Deliverable (or output). A specialist product that is handed over to the user(s).

Deterministic. Something with an outcome that is already known, with no possibility of that outcome changing.

Earliest start date. The earliest possible date when an activity can start within the logical and imposed constraints of the network.

Earned Value (EV). The value of completed work expressed in terms of the budget assigned to that work.

Earned Value Management (EVM). A best practice project control process that is based on a structured approach to planning, cost collection and performance measurement. It facilitates the integration of project scope, schedule, cost, risk and resource objectives and the establishment of a baseline plan for performance measurement.

Emergent risks. Those risks that have been identified through early warning indicators and trend analysis but require more development before being approved by the project board.

Enterprise. The aggregation of project, programme, Business As Usual and Portfolio activities within an organisation that make up its business.

Estimate. An approximation of project time and cost targets, refined throughout the project lifecycle.

Free float. The time by which an activity may be either delayed or extended without affecting the start of any succeeding activity.

Independent authority. An individual, team, or organisation that has no link to the project, programme or BAU undergoing the maturity process and is not unduly or unfairly influenced by those within the organisation's management structure. Such an authority can be internal or external to the organisation, depending on the nature and context of the assessment.

Integrated Master Schedule (IMS). A schedule that is generated from other schedules, usually from different parts of the project contract supply chain. The result of the vertical and/or horizontal linking of these through key activities or milestones.

Key deliverables. Those items that are linked to the satisfaction of Key Requirements. If delivery of these key items is not met within time, cost or quality limits, then this will directly affect the delivery of the entire project or programme.

Latest finish date. The latest possible date by which an activity has to finish within the logical activity and those imposed constraints of the network, without affecting the total project duration.

Lag. In a network diagram, the minimum necessary lapse of time between the finish of one activity and the finish of an overlapping activity. The delay incurred between two specified activities. The delay can be either positive or negative. An event occurring at time $t+k(k>0)$ is said to lag behind event occurring at time t, the extent of the lag being k. An event occurring k time units before another may be regarded as having a negative lag.

Lessons learned. The identification of activities associated with the project that went well, those that could have been better, to recommend improvements applied in the future and to future projects.

Management Information System (MIS). A collection of tools and applications that is used to manipulate data from management products to enable decisions to be made about a specific project(s) or programme(s).

Management Reserve (MR). An amount of the total allocated budget withheld for management control purposes rather than designated for the achievement of a specific task or set of tasks. It is not a part of the Performance Measurement Baseline. Also known as contingency (see 'buffer').

Milestone. An activity of zero duration principally used to enhance the clarity of the programme structure.

Mitigation action (risk response). Actions that may be taken to bring a situation to a level where exposure to risk is acceptable to the organisation. These responses fall into a number of risk response categories.

Negative lag. Also known as lead time. See Lag.

Negative Float. Amount of time that the start or finish of any activity exceeds the time allowed.

Network diagram. Any schematic display of the logical relationships of project activities. Always drawn from left to right to reflect project chronology.

Organisational Breakdown Structure (OBS). A functionally oriented code established to identity the performance responsibility for work on a specific contract.

Partner. An organisation or business that has entered into a legally binding agreement to manage a contract between them. Distinct from a legal partnership.

Performance Measurement Baseline (PMB). The time-phased budget plan against which contract performance is measured. It is formed by the budgets assigned to scheduled control accounts and the applicable indirect budgets. For future effort, not planned to the control account level, the performance measurement baseline also includes budgets assigned to higher level WBS elements and undistributed budgets. It equals the total allocated budget less management reserve.

Planning. The process of identifying the means, resources and actions necessary to accomplish an objective.

Positive lag. See Lag.

Programme controls. The application of processes to measure programme performance against the programme plan, to enable variances to be identified and corrected, so that programme objectives are achieved.

Project controls. The application of processes to measure project performance against the project plan, to enable variances to be identified and corrected, so that project objectives are achieved.

Recurring elements. Those schedule elements that are by their nature not unique and are repeated more than once throughout the project or programme phases – for example, production, logistic support or BAU activities (security checks, governance reviews etc).

Responsibility Assignment Matrix (RAM). A depiction of the relationship between the Contract Work Breakdown Structure elements and the organisations assigned responsibility for ensuring their accomplishment.

Schedule. A schedule is the timetable for a project. It shows how project activities and milestones are planned over a period of time. It is often shown as either a milestone chart, Gantt chart or other bar chart, or a tabulated series of dates.

Scheduling. The process used to determine the overall project duration. This includes identification of activities and their logical dependencies, and estimating activity durations, taking into account requirements and availability of resources. Not to be confused with planning.

Schedule Risk Analysis (SRA). A technique used to understand the effect of project risks on the early and late start and finish dates of activities and milestones within the schedule. It is used as part of the buffer allocation process.

Schedule Variance (SV). A metric for the schedule performance on a programme. It is the difference between earned value and the budget (Schedule Variance = Earned Value – Budget). A positive value is a favourable condition while a negative value is unfavourable.

Significant variances. Those differences between planned and actual performance, which require further review, analysis, or action. Appropriate thresholds should be established as to the magnitude of variances that will automatically require variance analysis.

Stakeholder. Any individual, group or organisation that can affect, be affected by, or perceive itself to be affected by, an initiative (programme, project, activity, risk).

Steering board. A group, usually comprising the sponsor, senior managers and sometimes key stakeholders, whose remit is to set the strategic direction of the project. It gives guidance to the project manager. Often referred to as the Steering Group or Project Board.

Supplier*. The person, group or groups responsible for the supply of the project's specialist products.

Total float. The time by which an activity may be either delayed or extended without affecting either the total project duration or violating a target finish date.

Uncertainty. A state of incomplete knowledge about a proposition. Usually associated with risks, both threats and opportunities.

Variances. See Significant Variances.

Work Breakdown Structure (WBS). A product-oriented family tree division of hardware, software, services and other work tasks which organises, defines, and graphically displays the product to be produced as well as the work to be completed to achieve the specified product.

Annex C – Abbreviations and acronyms

ANSI	American National Standards Institute
APM	Association For Project Management
BAU	Business As Usual
BOE	Basis Of Estimate
CAM	Control Account Manager
CPA	Critical Path Analysis
EVM	Earned Value Management
IMS	Integrated Master Schedule
ITPC	Introduction To Project Controls
LFE	Learning From Experience
LOB	Line Of Balance
MIS	Management Information System
MR	Management Reserve
NEC3	New Engineering Contract 3
OBS	Organisational Breakdown Structure
PMB	Performance Measurement Baseline
RAM	Responsibility Assignment Matrix
SIG	Specific Interest Group
SRA	Schedule Risk Analysis
SMM	Schedule Maturity Model
SV	Schedule Variance
VAR	Variance Analysis Report
WBS	Work Breakdown Structure

Annex D – Related Documents

In using the APM Scheduling Maturity Model the following documents provide additional information.

1. The Earned Value Management Compass, 2010, The Association for Project Management, ISBN: 978-1-903494-33-2
2. Earned Value Management APM Guidelines, 2008
   SBN: 978-1-903494-26-4
3. APM Introduction to Project Planning, 2008
   ISBN: 978-1-903494-28-8
4. APM Introduction to Project Control, 2010
   ISBN: 978-1-903494-34-9
5. APM Guide to Interfacing Risk and Earned Value Management, 2008
   ISBN: 978-1-903494-24-0